THE STORY-TELLER

EACH SAW THAT THE OTHER WAS HIS BROTHER.

THE STORY-TELLER

by · MAUD · LINDSAY

ILLUSTRATED · BY · FLORENCE · LILEY · YOUNG ·

BOSTON
· LOTHROP LEE & SHEPARD CO. ·

c1915
ETR

Published, August, 1915

NORWOOD PRESS
BERWICK & SMITH CO.
Norwood, Mass.
U. S. A.

To my cousin

Judith Winston Sherrod
in whose joyous company I journeyed
through the wonderland of youth

INTRODUCTION

I T was a glad day in the olden time when the Story-Teller came to cottage or hall. At Christmas, or New Year; when the May-pole stood on the village green; or the chestnuts were roasting in the coals on All-hallows eve; come when he would, he was always welcome; and if, when he was least expected, he knocked at the door, what joy there was!

Many were the miles that the Story-Teller had traveled, and many were the places where he had been; and many were the tales he had to tell of what he had seen and what he had heard in the wide world.

Sometimes his voice was deep and sweet as the organ in church on Sunday; and sometimes it rang out clear as a bugle; and sometimes as the tale went on he

7

would take the harp which was ever by his side; and touching it with skilful fingers, would weave a gay little song or a tender strain of music into his story, like a jeweled thread in a golden web.

All the children gathered around him, sturdy Gilbert and rosy Jocelyn, roguish Giles and slender Rosalind, eager for a story. Mother and father drew near, and in the background stood the servants, smiling but silent. Oh, everything was still as the house at midnight as the Story-Teller began his magic words: "Once upon a time."

Perhaps the story brought with it laughter, or perhaps a tear, but Life, said the Story-Teller, is made up of smiles and tears; and the little ones, listening to him, learned to rejoice with those whose joy was great, and to mourn with the sorrowful; and were the better and not the worse for it. And so in due time grew into noble men and good women.

It is many and many a year since they lived and

died; but still—knock, knock, knock—the Story-Teller comes with his harp and his story to every child's heart to-day.

Open the door and let him come in, give him a seat by the fire and gather close about him. And then you shall hear!

MAUD LINDSAY.

Sheffield, Alabama.

THE STORIES

11

ILLUSTRATIONS

13

THE STORY-TELLER

THE TWO BROTHERS

ONCE upon a time there lived two brothers, who, when they were children, were so seldom apart that those who saw one always looked for the other at his heels.

But when they had grown to manhood, and the time had come when they must make their own fortunes, the elder brother said to the younger:

"Choose as you will what you shall do, and God bless your choice; but as for me I shall make haste to the court of the king, for nothing will satisfy me but to serve him and my country."

"Good fortune and a blessing go with you," said the

younger brother. " I, too, should like to serve my country and the king, but I have neither words nor wit for a king's court. To hammer a shoe from the glowing iron while the red fire roars and the anvil rings—this is the work that I do best, and I shall be a blacksmith, even as my father was before me."

So when he had spoken the two brothers embraced and bade each other good-bye and went on their ways; nor did they meet again till many a year had come and gone.

The elder brother rode to the king's court just as he had said he would; and as time went on he won great honor there and was made one of the king's counselors.

And the younger brother built himself a blacksmith's shop by the side of a road and worked there merrily from early morn till the stars shone at night. He was called the Mighty Blacksmith because of his strength, and the Honest Blacksmith because he charged no more than his work was worth, and the

Master Blacksmith because no other smith in the coun-
tryside could shoe a horse so well and speedily as he.
And he was envious of nobody, for always as he worked
his hammer seemed to sing to him :

> " Cling, clang, cling ! Cling, clang, cling !
> He who does his very best,
> Is fit to serve the king."

Now in those days news came to the king of the
country where the two brothers lived that the duke of
the next kingdom had made threats against him, and
against his people; and there was great excitement in
the land.

Some of the king's counselors wanted him to gather
his armies and march at once into the duke's kingdom.

"If we do not make war upon him, he will make
war upon us," they said.

But some of the king's counselors loved peace, and
among these was the elder brother, in whom the king
had great trust.

"Let me, I pray you, ride to the duke's castle," he said to the king, "that we may learn from his own lips if he is friend or foe, for much is told that is not true; and it is easier to begin a fight than it is to end one."

The king was well pleased with all the elder brother said, and bade him go.

"But if by the peal of the noon bells on the day before Christmas you have neither brought nor sent a message of good will from the duke to me, then shall those who want war have their way," he said, and with this the elder brother had to be content.

Day and night he rode to the duke's castle, and day and night, when his errand was done, he hastened home again. But the way was long and a strong wind had blown away the sign-posts which guided travelers, so, though he stopped neither to sleep in a bed or eat at a table the whole journey through, the early hours of the day before Christmas found him still far from the king's palace.

And to make matters worse, in the loneliest part of the road, the good horse, that had carried him so well, lost a shoe.

> " Alack and alas ! for the want of a nail
> The horseshoe is lost; and my good horse will fail
> For the want of the shoe ; and I shall be late
> For want of a steed ; and my message must wait
> For want of a bearer ; and woe is our plight,
> For want of the message the king needs must fight!"[1]

cried the elder brother then ; and he bowed his head upon his saddle and wept, for where to turn for help he did not know.

The sun had not yet risen and no other traveler was on the road, nor could he see through the dim light of dawn a house or watch-tower where he might ask aid. But as he wept he heard a distant sound that was sweeter than music to his ears :

> " Cling, clang, cling !   Cling, clang, cling ! "

[1] Adapted from the old proverb, " For want of a nail, the shoe was lost," etc.

"Only a blacksmith plays that tune!" he cried; and he urged his horse on joyfully, calling as he went:

"Smith, smith, if you love country and king, shoe my horse, and shoe him speedily."

It was not long before he spied the fire of a roadside smithy glaring out upon him like a great red eye, and when he reached the door of the shop he found the smith ready and waiting for his task.

Cling, clang, cling! How the iron rang beneath his mighty stroke! And cling, clang, cling, how the hammer sang as the shoe was pounded into shape!

By the time the sun was over the hill the horse was shod, and the rider was in his saddle again.

But the blacksmith would take no money for his work.

"To serve my country and the king is pay enough for me," he said; and he stood up straight and tall and looked the king's counselor in the eyes.

And lo! and behold, as the morning light fell on their faces, each saw that the other was his brother.

"God bless you, brother," and "God speed you, brother," was all that they had time to say, but that was enough to show that love was still warm in their hearts.

Then away, and away, and away, through the sun and the dew rode the elder brother—away and away over hill and dale toward the king's palace.

The king and his counselors were watching and waiting there, and as the sun climbed high and the message did not come, those who wanted war said:

"Shall we not saddle our horses, and call up our men?"

"The bells in the steeple have yet to ring for noon," said the peace-lovers; "and we see a dust on the king's highway."

"Dust flies before wind," said the warriors, "and it is likelier that our messenger lies in the duke's prison than rides on the king's highway."

But with the dust came the sound of flying hoofs.
Faster, faster, faster, they came.   When the first stroke
of the noon hour pealed from the church steeple the
king's messenger was in sight, and the last bell had
not rung when he stood before the palace gate to de-
liver the duke's message :

> " Peace and good will to you and yours ;
> And to all a Merry Christmas."

Then the king sent for fine robes and a golden chain
to be brought for the elder brother, and put a purse of
gold in his hand, for he was well pleased with what
he had done.

But the elder brother would have none of these
things for himself alone.

" Try as I would, I must have failed had it not been
for my brother, the blacksmith, who shod my horse
on the road to-day," he said ; " and, if it please your
majesty, half of all you give to me I will give to him."

" Two good servants are better than one," said the king, and he sent for the younger brother that he might thank him also.

Then the two brothers were clothed alike and feasted alike, and each had a purse of gold; and whenever one was praised, so was the other.

And they lived happily, each in his own work, all the days of their lives.

THE JAR OF ROSEMARY

THERE was once a little prince whose mother, the queen, was sick. All summer she lay in bed, and everything was kept quiet in the palace; but when the autumn came she grew better. Every day brought color to her cheeks, and strength to her limbs, and by and by the little prince was allowed to go into her room and stand beside her bed to talk to her.

He was very glad of this for he wanted to ask her what she would like for a Christmas present; and as soon as he had kissed her, and laid his cheek against hers, he whispered his question in her ear.

"What should I like for a Christmas present?" said the queen. "A smile and a kiss and a hug around the neck; these are the dearest gifts I know."

But the prince was not satisfied with this answer. "Smiles and kisses and hugs you can have every day," he said, "but think, mother, think, if you could choose the thing you wanted most in all the world what would you take?"

So the queen thought and thought, and at last she said:

"If I might take my choice of all the world I believe a little jar of rosemary like that which bloomed in my mother's window when I was a little girl would please me better than anything else."

The little prince was delighted to hear this, and as soon as he had gone out of the queen's room he sent a servant to his father's greenhouses to inquire for a rosemary plant.

But the servant came back with disappointing news. There were carnation pinks in the king's greenhouses, and roses with golden hearts, and lovely lilies; but there was no rosemary. Rosemary was a common herb and grew, mostly, in country gardens, so the king's gardeners said.

"Then go into the country for it," said the little prince. "No matter where it grows, my mother must have it for a Christmas present."

So messengers went into the country here, there, and everywhere to seek the plant, but each one came back with the same story to tell; there was rosemary, enough and to spare, in the spring, but the frost had been in the country and there was not a green sprig left to bring to the little prince for his mother's Christmas present.

Two days before Christmas, however, news was brought that rosemary had been found, a lovely green plant growing in a jar, right in the very city where the prince himself lived.

"But where is it?" said he. "Why have you not brought it with you? Go and get it at once."

"Well, as for that," said the servant who had found

the plant, "there is a little difficulty. The old woman to whom the rosemary belongs did not want to sell it even though I offered her a handful of silver for it."

"Then give her a purse of gold," said the little prince.

So a purse filled so full of gold that it could not hold another piece was taken to the old woman; but presently it was brought back. She would not sell her rosemary; no, not even for a purse of gold.

"Perhaps if your little highness would go yourself and ask her, she might change her mind," said the prince's nurse. So the royal carriage drawn by six white horses was brought, and the little prince and his servants rode away to the old woman's house, and when they got there the first thing they spied was the little green plant in a jar standing in the old woman's window.

The old woman, herself, came to the door, and she was glad to see the little prince. She invited him in, and bade him warm his hands by the fire, and gave him a cooky from her cupboard to eat.

She had a little grandson no older than the prince, but he was sick and could not run about and play like other children. He lay in a little white bed in the old woman's room, and the little prince, after he had eaten the cooky, spoke to him, and took out his favorite plaything, which he always carried in his pocket, and showed it to him.

The prince's favorite plaything was a ball which was like no other ball that had ever been made. It was woven of magic stuff as bright as the sunlight, as sparkling as the starlight, and as golden as the moon at harvest time. And when the little prince threw it into the air, or bounced it on the floor or turned it in his hands it rang like a chime of silver bells.

The sick child laughed to hear it, and held out his hands for it, and the prince let him hold it, which pleased the grandmother as much as the child.

But pleased though she was she would not sell the rosemary. She had brought it from the home where she had lived when her little grandson's father was a boy, she said, and she hoped to keep it till she died. So the prince and his servants had to go home without it.

No sooner had they gone than the sick child began to talk of the wonderfull ball.

"If I had such a ball to hold in my hand," he said, " I should be contented all the day."

"You may as well wish for the moon in the sky," said his grandmother; but she thought of what he said, and in the evening when he was asleep she put her shawl around her, and taking the jar of rosemary with her she hastened to the king's palace.

When she got there the servants asked her errand but she would answer nothing till they had taken her to the little prince.

"Silver and gold would not buy the rosemary," she

said when she saw him; "but if you will give me your golden ball for my little grandchild you may have the plant."

"But my ball is the most wonderful ball that was ever made!" cried the little prince; "and it is my favorite plaything. I would not give it away for anything."

And so the old woman had to go home with her jar of rosemary under her shawl.

The next day was the day before Christmas and there was a great stir and bustle in the palace. The queen's physician had said that she might sit up to see the Christmas Tree that night, and have her presents with the rest of the family; and every one was running to and fro to get things in readiness for her.

The queen had so many presents, and very fine they were, too, that the Christmas Tree could not hold them all, so they were put on a table before the throne and wreathed around with holly and with pine. The little prince went in with his nurse to see them, and to put his gift, which was a jewel, among them.

"She wanted a jar of rosemary," he said as he looked at the glittering heap.

"She will never think of it again when she sees these things.   You may be sure of that," said the nurse.

But the little prince was not sure.   He thought of it himself many times that day, and once, when he was playing with his ball, he said to the nurse:

"If I had a rosemary plant I'd be willing to sell it for a purse full of gold.   Wouldn't you?"

"Indeed, yes," said the nurse; "and so would any one else in his right senses.   You may be sure of that."

The little boy was not satisfied, though, and presently when he had put his ball up and stood at the window watching the snow which had come to whiten the earth for Christ's birthday, he said to the nurse:

"I wish it were spring.   It is easy to get rosemary then, is it not?"

" Your little highness is like the king's parrot that knows but one word with your rosemary, rosemary, rosemary," said the nurse who was a little out of patience by that time. " Her majesty, the queen, only asked for it to please you. You may be sure of that."

But the little prince was not sure; and when the nurse had gone to her supper and he was left by chance for a moment alone, he put on his coat of fur, and taking the ball with him he slipped away from the palace, and hastened toward the old woman's house.

He had never been out at night by himself before, and he might have felt a little afraid had it not been for the friendly stars that twinkled in the sky above him.

" We will show you the way," they seemed to say; and he trudged on bravely in their light, till, by and by, he came to the house and knocked at the door.

Now the little sick child had been talking of the

SHE TOOK THE LITTLE PRINCE IN HER ARMS
AND KISSED HIM.

wonderful ball all the evening. "Did you see how it shone, grandmother? And did you hear how the little bells rang?" he said; and it was just then that the little prince knocked at the door.

The old woman made haste to answer the knock and when she saw the prince she was too astonished to speak.

"Here is the ball," he cried, putting it into her hands. "Please give me the rosemary for my mother."

And so it happened that when the queen sat down before her great table of gifts the first thing she spied was a jar of sweet rosemary like that which had bloomed in her mother's window when she was a little girl.

"I should rather have it than all the other gifts in the world," she said; and she took the little prince in her arms and kissed him.

THE PROMISE[1]

A Christmas Wonder Story for Older Children

THERE was once a harper who played such beautiful music and sang such beautiful songs that his fame spread throughout the whole land; and at last the king heard of him and sent messengers to bring him to the palace.

"I will neither eat nor sleep till I have seen your face and heard the sound of your harp." This was the message the king sent to the harper.

The messengers said it over and over until they knew it by heart, and when they reached the harper's house they called:

[1] This story was suggested by an old poem, told to me by Miss Harriette Mills, which recounted the adventures of a father who braved the snows of an Alpine pass to reach his home on Christmas day.

" Hail, harper ! Come out and listen, for we have something to tell you that will make you glad."

But when the harper heard the king's message he was sad, for he had a wife and a child and a little brown dog; and he was sorry to leave them and they were sorry to have him go.

" Stay with us," they begged ; but the harper said :

" I *must* go, for it would be discourtesy to disappoint the king ; but as sure as holly berries are red and pine is green, I will come back by Christmas day to eat my share of the Christmas pudding, and sing the Christmas songs by my own fireside."

And when he had promised this he hung his harp upon his back and went away with the messengers to the king's palace.

When he got there the king welcomed him with joy, and many things were done in his honor. He slept on a bed of softest down, and ate from a plate of gold at the king's own table ; and when he sang everybody and everything, from the king himself to the mouse in the palace pantry, stood still to listen.

No matter what he was doing, however, feasting or resting, singing or listening to praises, he never forgot the promise that he had made to his wife and his child and his little brown dog; and when the day before Christmas came, he took his harp in his hand and went to bid the king good-bye.

Now the king was loath to have the harper leave him, and he said to him:

"I will give you a horse that is white as milk, as glossy as satin, and fleet as a deer, if you will stay to play and sing before my throne on Christmas day."

But the harper answered, "I cannot stay, for I have a wife and a child and a little brown dog; and I have promised them to be at home by Christmas day to eat my share of the Christmas pudding and sing the Christmas songs by my own fireside."

Then the king said, "If you will stay to play and

sing before my throne on Christmas day I will give to you a wonderful tree that summer or winter is never bare; and silver and gold will fall for you whenever you shake this little tree."

But the harper said, " I must not stay, for my wife and my child and my little brown dog are waiting for me, and I have promised them to be at home by Christmas day to eat my share of the Christmas pudding and sing the Christmas songs by my own fireside."

Then the king said, " If you will stay on Christmas day one tune to play and one song to sing, I will give you a velvet robe to wear, and you may sit beside me here with a ring on your finger and a crown on your head."

But the harper answered, " I *will* not stay, for my wife and my child and my little brown dog are watching for me; and I have promised them to be at home by Christmas day to eat my share of the Christmas pudding and sing the Christmas songs by my own fireside." And he wrapped his old cloak about him, and hung his harp upon his back, and went out from the king's palace without another word.

He had not gone far when the little white snow-flakes came fluttering down from the skies.

> "Harper, stay," they seemed to say,
> "Do not venture out to-day."

But the harper said, "The snow may fall, but I must go, for I have a wife and a child and a little brown dog; and I have promised them to be at home by Christmas day to eat my share of the Christmas pudding and sing the Christmas songs by my own fireside."

Then the snow fell thick, and the snow fell fast. The hills and the valleys, the hedges and hollows were white. The paths were all hidden, and there were drifts like mountains on the king's highway. The harper stumbled and the harper fell, but he would not turn back; and as he traveled he met the wind.

> "Brother Harper, turn, I pray;
> Do not journey on to-day,"

sang the wind, but the harper would not heed.

"Snows may fall and winds may blow, but I must go on," he said, "for I have a wife and a child and a little brown dog; and I have promised them to be at home by Christmas day to eat my share of the Christmas pudding and sing the Christmas songs by my own fireside."

Then the wind blew an icy blast. The snow froze on the ground and the water froze in the rivers. The harper's breath froze in the air, and icicles as long as the king's sword hung from the rocks on the king's highway. The harper shivered and the harper shook, but he would not turn back; and by and by he came to the forest that lay between him and his home.

The trees of the forest were creaking and bending in the wind, and every one of them seemed to say :

> " Darkness gathers, night is near ;
> Harper, stop ! Don't venture here."

But the harper would not stop. "Snows may fall, winds may blow, and night may come, but I have promised to be at home by Christmas day to eat my share of the Christmas pudding and sing the Christmas songs by my own fireside. I must go on."

And on he went till the last glimmer of daylight faded, and there was darkness everywhere. But the harper was not afraid of the dark.

" If I cannot see I can sing," said he, and he sang in the forest joyously :

> " Sing glory, glory, glory !
> And bless God's holy name ;
> For 'twas on Christmas morning,
> The little Jesus came.

" He wore no robes; no crown of gold
　　Was on His head that morn;
But herald angels sang for joy,
　　To tell a King was born."

The snow ceased its falling, the wind ceased its blow-ing, the trees of the forest bowed down to listen, and, lo! dear children, as he sang the darkness turned to wondrous light, and close at hand the harper saw the open doorway of his home.

The wife and the child and the little brown dog were watching and waiting, and they welcomed the harper with great joy. The holly berries were red in the Christmas wreaths; their Christmas tree was a young green pine; the Christmas pudding was full of plums; and the harper was happier than a king as he sat by his own fireside to sing:

" O glory, glory, glory!
　　We praise God's holy name;
For 'twas to bring His wondrous love,
　　The little Jesus came.

" And in our hearts it shines anew,
While at His throne we pray,
God bless us all for Jesus' sake,
This happy Christmas day."

THE HARPER'S SONG

Words, MAUD LINDSAY   Music, ELSIE A. MERRIMAN

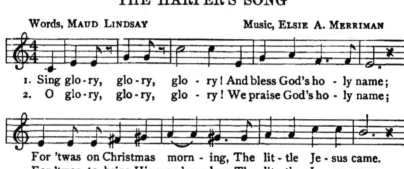

1. Sing glo-ry, glo-ry, glo - ry! And bless God's ho - ly name;
2. O glo-ry, glo-ry, glo - ry! We praise God's ho - ly name;

For 'twas on Christmas morn - ing, The lit - tle Je - sus came.
For 'twas to bring His wondrous love, The lit - tle Je - sus came.

He wore no robes; no crown of gold Was on His head that morn; But
And in our hearts it shines a-new, While at His throne we pray, God

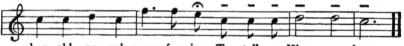

her - ald an - gels sang for joy, To tell a King was born.
bless us all for Je - sus' sake, This hap - py Christ - mas day.

THE PLATE OF PANCAKES

ONCE upon a time a woman was frying some pancakes, and as she turned the last cake in the pan she said to her little boy :

"If you were a little older I should send you with some of these fine cakes for your father's dinner, but as it is, he must wait till supper for them."

"Oh, do let me take them," said the little boy, whose name was Karl. "Just see how tall I am. And only yesterday my grandmother said I was old enough to learn my letters. Do let me go!"

And he begged and begged till at last she selected the brownest and crispest cakes, and putting them in a plate with a white napkin over them she bade him take them.

Now the path that led from Karl's home to the saw-mill where his father worked was straight enough, and plain enough, but it ran through the wood that was called Enchanted. Fairies lived there, so some people thought, and goblins that liked to work mischief; and never before had the little boy been allowed to go there alone.

As he hurried along with the plate of pancakes in his hand he glanced into every green thicket that he passed, half hopeful, and half fearful that he might find a tiny creature hidden in the leaves. Not a glimpse of fairy or goblin did he see, but when he came to the blackberry bushes where the sweetest berries grow something seemed to whisper to him: "Stop, Karl, and eat."

"But I am taking a plate of pancakes for my father's dinner," said Karl speaking aloud.

"A moment or two will make no difference. You can run fast," came the whisper again.

"Oh, yes, I can run fast," said Karl; and he put the plate down under the bushes and began to pick

SOMETHING SEEMED TO WHISPER TO HIM:
"STOP, KARL, AND EAT."

the berries. They were as ripe and sweet as they had looked and every one that the little boy put into his mouth made him wish for another; and if he turned away from the bushes the whisper was sure to come: " One more and then go."

The pancakes grew cold in the plate, and the sun which had been high in the sky when Karl started from home slipped farther and farther into the west; but still he lingered, till suddenly the evening whistle of the mill sounded sharp and shrill in his ears.

" Why, it is time for my father to come home," he cried. " Dear me, dear me, what shall I do? "

There was nothing for him to do but to go home, so home he went with the plate of cold pancakes in his hand and the tears rolling down his cheeks.

When he told his mother and grandmother what had happened they looked at each other wisely as if they thought more about it than they would say; but they bade him dry his tears.

"You will be more careful another time," they said; and so the matter ended.

But Karl did not forget it. It was many a month before his mother fried pancakes again, but no sooner did he see her turning the cakes in the pan than he said:

"I wish my father had some of these fine cakes for his dinner, don't you, mother?"

"Indeed I do," said she, smiling at his grandmother as she spoke; and as soon as the cakes were done she selected the brownest and crispest, and putting them in a plate with a white napkin over them, she bade him take them.

"I'll get there in time for my father's dinner to-day," he said as he started out; but in a very short while he was back with an empty plate in his hand, and the tears rolling down his cheeks.

"I only put the plate down for a minute while I chased a rabbit that said, 'If you catch me you may have me;' and when I came back every pancake was gone," he sobbed.

His mother and grandmother looked at each other wisely when they heard this.

"It is just as I thought the first time," said his mother. "The goblins are at work in the wood. He must never go there again."

But to this the grandmother would not agree.

"Leave it to me," she said, and the very next day she fried pancakes, and selecting the brownest and crispest she put them in a plate with a white napkin over them and bade Karl take them to his father.

"And if any bid you stop or stay, or turn your feet from out your way, say but the word that is spelled with the fourteenth and fifteenth letters of the alphabet three times in a loud voice, and all will go well with you," she said.

"All right," said Karl, nodding his head proudly, for he knew all his letters by this time and could spell hard words like c-a-t, cat, m-a-t, mat. "All right," but he did not stop to count the letters then for he was in a great hurry to be off.

"I guess my father will be glad to get such fine pancakes for his dinner," he said ; and he ran so fast that he was half-way to the mill before he knew it.

There was no whispering voice in the wood that day and no talking rabbit to tempt him to a chase ; but as he came to a place where another path crossed his own, a bird called out from the heart of the wood :

"Quick, quick, come here, here, here——"

"Where, where?" cried Karl ; and he was just about to start in search of the bird when he remembered what his grandmother had said :

"If any bid you stop or stay, or turn your feet from out your way, say but the word that is spelled with the fourteenth and fifteenth letters of the alphabet three times in a loud voice, and all will go well with you."

"A, B, C, D, E, F, G," he chanted, counting the letters on his fingers as he said them, "H, I, J, K, L, M, N, O:" N was the fourteenth letter and O was the fifteenth. N-O; that was easy.

"No! No! No!" he shouted; and—do you believe it?—in less time than it takes to tell it he was at the mill door with every pancake safe and hot.

And the story goes that though he came and went through the Enchanted Wood all the days of his life he was never hindered by anything there again; and he never saw a goblin though he lived to be as old as his grandmother had been when he was a little boy.

LITTLE MAID HILDEGARDE

ONE evening Little Maid Hildegarde's father came home with wonderful news; the knights were coming to town. He had heard it as he came from the forest where he cut wood all day and he hurried every step of the way home to tell Hildegarde and her mother.

"They are on the king's business and will be at the Church Square to-morrow morning at the hour of ten. Everybody in town will be there to see them. Old Grandmother Grey is going to ask them to ride in search of her little lamb that has gone astray; and the mayor will tell them of the wolves that come in the winter. The good knights are always glad to help," he said.

Little Maid Hildegarde knew all about the knights.
Her father was never tired of telling, or she of hearing,
how they fought and killed the fierce dragon that had
troubled the people of the border; and put out the
forest fires in the time of the great drought and
fed the hungry when the famine was in the land.
And yet with all of their great deeds they were
merry men, not too proud to sing at a feast or play
with a child.

And many an evening, though Hildegarde was growing to be a great girl, her mother sat by her bed to sing
a song that she had sung to her when she was a babe
in the cradle :

> " Hush, my baby, do not cry,
> Five brave knights go riding by.
> One is dressed in bonny blue ;
> He's the leader, strong and true.
> One is clad from head to toe
> In an armor white as snow.

One in crimson bright is drest,
With a star upon his breast.
One in gold and one in green,
Cloth of gold and satin sheen.
Hush, my baby, do not cry,
Five brave knights go riding by."

Oh, how Hildegarde had longed to see those splendid riders! And now at last she was to have her heart's desire. It seemed almost too good to be true.

"Shall we start to town as soon as the new day comes?" she asked.

"Just as soon as the cows are taken to the pasture, and the little chicks are fed," said her mother; and the little maid went to bed well satisfied.

But alas, for Hildegarde and her hopes! The morning sun had scarcely shone when her mother awoke with a terrible pain in her head, and her father slipped on his way to the barn and sprained his foot so he could not walk. And there was no one to take the child to the Church Square. No, not even a neighbor, for Hildegarde and her mother and father lived apart from every one else, and the wood that is called Enchanted lay between them and the town.

There was no help for it. Hildegarde knew herself, without a word from any one, that she could not go; but as she ran about the house to wait on them, she heard her mother and father talking.

"It is not for the pain in my face that I grieve," said the good mother; "but for the disappointment of our little maid."

"Aye," said the father, "I would bear my hurt, and more too, willingly, if only she might see the gallant knights."

And when Hildegarde heard what they said she made haste to wipe away the tears that threatened to roll down her cheeks, and went about her work with a pleasant face.

All day long she was busy for there were the cows

to take to the pasture, and the little chicks to feed, and the eggs to gather ; but at sunset her tasks were done, and with her doll in her arms she sat in the doorway of the house and looked away toward the town, the towers of which just showed above the Enchanted Wood.

Highest of all was the spire of the church that stood in the square where the knights had been ; and as Hildegarde watched it change from grey to gold in the sunset glow, she thought of them and wondered where they had gone when their business was done.

Some day they would come again and then she should surely see them, her father said ; and already she had begun to look forward to that time.

" Perhaps they will come when the wolves do in the winter," she said to herself; but scarcely had she spoken when through an opening in the wood she spied a horseman riding at a stately pace. Behind him came another, and another till she had counted five—

five brave knights ! Yes, there they came with prancing steeds and shining shields, and splendid clothes !

One bore a banner blue as the sky on a summer's day, and the next held a wee lamb close within his arms. A dragon's head hung from another's saddle, and two had bugles by their sides.

Not a word was spoken. As silently as the stars shine out at evening they passed the door where the child sat wonder-struck ; and as quietly as the sun goes down at the day's end they vanished into the wood again before she could move or call. But just as the green of the last one's coat faded away into the green of the trees, Hildegarde thought she heard a strain of sweetest music !

Now there were those, and Hildegarde's mother and father were among them, who believed that the little maid, tired from her long busy day, had fallen asleep, and dreamed a beautiful dream.

But as for Hildegarde, she kept the vision in her heart alway ; and when as the years went by she had little ones of her own to rock to sleep, she told them of it, and sang to them as her mother had sung to her:

FIVE BRAVE KNIGHTS

Words, MAUD LINDSAY   Air, Old Song

Hush, my ba-by, do not cry, Five brave knights go rid-ing by.

One is dressed in bon-ny blue; He's the lead-er, strong and true.

One is clad from head to toe In an ar-mor white as snow.

One in crim-son bright is drest, With a star up-on his breast.

One in gold and one in green, Cloth of gold and sat-in sheen.

Hush, my ba-by, do not cry, Five brave knights go rid-ing by.

YES, THERE THEY CAME!

THE APPLE DUMPLING

THERE was once upon a time an old woman who wanted an apple dumpling for supper. She had plenty of flour and plenty of butter, plenty of sugar and plenty of spice for a dozen dumplings, but there was one thing she did not have; and that was an apple.

She had plums, a tree full of them, the roundest and reddest that you can imagine; but, though you can make butter from cream and raisins of grapes, you cannot make an apple dumpling with plums, and there is no use trying.

The more the old woman thought of the dumpling the more she wanted it, and at last she dressed herself in her Sunday best and started out to seek an apple.

Before she left home, however, she filled a basket

with plums from her plum-tree and, covering it over with a white cloth, hung it on her arm, for she said to herself: "There may be those in the world who have apples, and need plums."

She had not gone very far when she came to a poultry yard filled with fine hens and geese and guineas. Ca-ca, quawk, quawk, poterack! What a noise they made; and in the midst of them stood a young woman who was feeding them with yellow corn. She nodded pleasantly to the old woman, and the old woman nodded to her; and soon the two were talking as if they had known each other always.

The young woman told the old woman about her fowls and the old woman told the young woman about the dumpling and the basket of plums for which she hoped to get apples.

"Dear me," said the young woman when she heard this, "there is nothing my husband likes better than plum jelly with goose for his Sunday dinner, but unless you will take a bag of feathers for your plums he must do without, for that is the best I can offer you."

" One pleased is better than two disappointed," said the old woman then; and she emptied the plums into the young woman's apron and putting the bag of feathers into her basket trudged on as merrily as before; for she said to herself:

" If I am no nearer the dumpling than when I left home, I am at least no farther from it; and that feathers are lighter to carry than plums nobody can deny."

Trudge, trudge, up hill and down she went, and presently she came to a garden of sweet flowers; lilies, lilacs, violets, roses—oh, never was there a lovelier garden !

The old woman stopped at the gate to look at the flowers; and as she looked she heard a man and a woman, who sat on the door-step of a house that stood in the garden, quarreling.

" Cotton," said the woman.

" Straw," said the man.

" 'Tis not ——"

" It is," they cried, and so it went between them, till they spied the old woman at the gate.

" Here is one who will settle the matter," said the woman then ; and she called to the old woman :

" Good mother, answer me this : If you were making a cushion for your grandfather's chair would you not stuff it with cotton ? "

" No," said the old woman.

" I told you so," cried the man. " Straw is the thing, and no need to go farther than the barn for it ; " but the old woman shook her head.

" I would not stuff the cushion with straw," said she ; and it would have been hard to tell which one was the more cast down by her answers, the man or the woman.

But the old woman made haste to take the bag of feathers out of her basket, and give it to them.

" A feather cushion is fit for a king," she said, " and as for me, an apple for a dumpling, or a nosegay from your garden will serve me as well as what I give."

The man and the woman had no apples, but they were glad to exchange a nosegay from their garden for a bag of fine feathers, you may be sure.

" There is nothing nicer for a cushion than feathers," said the woman.

" My mother had one made of them," said the man ; and they laughed like children as they hurried into the garden to fill the old woman's basket with the loveliest posies ; lilies, lilacs, violets, roses—oh ! never was there a sweeter nosegay.

" A good bargain, and not all of it in the basket," said the old woman, for she was pleased to have stopped the quarrel, and when she had wished the two good fortune and a long life, she went upon her way again.

Now her way was the king's highway, and as she walked there she met a young lord who was dressed in his finest clothes, for he was going to see his lady love. He would have been as handsome a young man as ever the sun shone on had it not been that his forehead was wrinkled into a terrible frown, and the corners of his mouth drawn down as if he had not a friend left in the whole world.

"A fair day and a good road," said the old woman, stopping to drop him a courtesy.

"Fair or foul, good or bad, 'tis all one to me," said he, " when the court jeweler has forgotten to send the ring he promised, and I must go to my lady with empty hands."

"Empty hands are better than an empty heart," said the old woman; "but then we are young only once; so you shall have a gift for your lady though I may never have an apple dumpling." And she took the nosegay from her basket and gave it to the young lord which pleased him so much that the frown smoothed away from his forehead, and his mouth spread itself in a smile, and he was as handsome a young man as ever the sun shone on.

"Fair exchange is no robbery,"[1] said he, and he unfastened a golden chain from round his neck and gave it to the old woman, and went away holding his nosegay with great care.

The old woman was delighted.

"With this golden chain I might buy all the apples in the king's market, and then have something to spare," she said to herself, as she hurried away toward town as fast as her feet could carry her.

But she had gone no farther than the turn of the road when she came upon a mother and children, standing in a doorway, whose faces were as sorrowful as her own was happy.

"What is the matter?" she asked as soon as she reached them.

"Matter enough," answered the mother, "when the

[1] An old saying.

last crust of bread is eaten and not a farthing in the house to buy more."

"Well-a-day," cried the old woman when this was told her. "Never shall it be said of me that I eat apple dumpling for supper while my neighbors lack bread;" and she put the golden chain into the mother's hands and hurried on without waiting for thanks.

She was not out of sight of the house, though, when the mother and children, every one of them laughing and talking as if it were Christmas or Candlemas day, overtook her.

"Little have we to give you," said the mother who was the happiest of all, "for that you have done for us, but here is a little dog, whose barking will keep loneliness from your house, and a blessing goes with it."

The old woman did not have the heart to say them nay, so into the basket went the little dog, and very snugly he lay there.

SHE SAW AN APPLE-TREE AS FULL OF APPLES AS
HER PLUM-TREE WAS FULL OF PLUMS.

" A bag of feathers for a basket of plums ; a nosegay of flowers for a bag of feathers ; a golden chain for a nosegay of flowers ; a dog and a blessing for a golden chain ; all the world is give and take, and who knows but that I may have my apple yet," said the old woman as she hurried on.

And sure enough she had not gone a half dozen yards when, right before her, she saw an apple-tree as full of apples as her plum-tree was full of plums. It grew in front of a house as much like her own as if the two were peas in the same pod ; and on the porch of the house sat a little old man.

" A fine tree of apples ! " called the old woman as soon as she was in speaking distance of him.

"Aye, but apple-trees and apples are poor company when a man is growing old," said the old man ; " and I would give them all if I had even so much as a little dog to bark on my door-step."

" Bow-wow ! " called the dog in the old woman's

basket, and in less time than it takes to read this story he was barking on the old man's door-step, and the old woman was on her way home with a basket of apples on her arm.

She got there in plenty of time to make the dumpling for supper, and it was as sweet and brown a dumpling as heart could desire.

"If you try long enough and hard enough you can always have an apple dumpling for supper," said the old woman; and she ate the dumpling to the very last crumb; and enjoyed it, too.

THE KING'S SERVANT[1]

THERE was once upon a time a faithful servant whose name was Hans. He served the king his master so long and so well that one day the king said to him:

"Speak, Hans, and tell me what three things do you most desire that I may give them to you as a reward for your faithfulness."

It did not take Hans long to answer the king.

"If you please, your majesty," he said, "I should like best in all the world to go to see my mother; to have a horse on which to ride upon my journey; and to taste the food that lies hidden in the silver dish that comes each day to your majesty's table."

And when the king heard this he made haste to send

[1] Adapted with a free hand from Grimm's "White Snake."

for the silver dish and lifting the lid with his own hand he bade Hans taste of the food inside. What this food was, neither I nor anybody else can tell you, but no sooner had Hans tasted it than he understood what everything in the world was saying, from the birds in the tree-tops to the hens in the king's poultry yard.

"Good-bye, Hans," they called as Hans mounted the horse which the king gave him and rode away through the gate.

"Good-bye," said Hans, and he cantered off in fine style down the king's highway.

Before he had ridden far, however, he heard such a moaning and complaining by the roadside that he stopped his horse to see what the matter was; and—do you believe it?—it was the ant people whose ant-hill stood in the way, right where Hans was about to ride.

"See, see!" they cried, running to and fro in great alarm. "This giant of a man on his terrible horse will ride over our new house and crush us to death."

"Not I," said Hans. "If so much as one of you gets under my horse's hoofs it will be your fault and not mine;" and getting down from his horse he led him around the ant-hill and into the road on the other side.

"One good turn deserves another," cried the ant people running to and fro in great joy. "You have helped us, and we will help you some day;" and they were still saying this when Hans mounted his horse and rode away.

Now before long Hans came to a great forest and as he rode under the spreading branches of the trees he heard a cry for help in the woods.

"What can this be?" said Hans; but the very next minute he saw two young birds lying beneath a tree, beating their wings upon the ground and crying aloud:

"Alas! Alas! Who will put us into the nest again?"

" I, the king's servant and my mother's son ; I will put you into the nest again," said Hans, and he was as good as his word.

"One good turn deserves another," called the birds when they were safe in their nest once more. " You have helped us, and we will help you some day."

Hans laughed to hear them, for though it was easy for him to help them he could not think what they might do for him.

Trot, trot, and gallop, gallop he rode through the forest till he came to a stream of water beside which lay three panting fishes.

"We shall surely die unless we can get into the water," they cried.

Their breath was almost gone and their voices were no louder than the faintest whisper, but Hans understood every word that they said ; and he jumped from his horse and threw them into the stream.

"One good turn deserves another," they cried as

they swam merrily away. "You have helped us, and we will help you some day."

Now it so happened that Hans came by and by to the land of a very wicked king who broke his promises as easily as if they were made of spun glass and who never thought of anybody but himself.

No sooner had Hans come into the land than the king stopped him and would not let him go on.

"No one shall pass through my kingdom," he said, "till he has done one piece of work for me."

Hans was not afraid of work. "Show it to me that I may do it at once," he said; "for I am hastening to see my mother."

Then the king took Hans into a room as large as a meadow where some of all the seeds in the world was stored. There were lettuce-seeds, and radish-seeds, flax-seeds and grains of rice, fine seeds of flowers and small seeds of grass, all mixed and mingled till no two alike lay together.

Hans had never seen so many seeds in all his life before; and when he had looked at them the king bade him sort them, each kind to itself.

"The lettuce-seed must be here, and the radish-seed there; the flax-seed in this corner and the grains of rice in another; the fine seeds of flowers must be in their place, and the small seeds of grass all ready for planting before you can pass through my kingdom and go on your way," he said; and when he had spoken he went out of the room and locked the door behind him.

Poor Hans! He sat down on the floor and cried— the tears rolled down his cheeks I do assure you—for he said to himself:

"If I live to be a hundred years old I can never do this thing that the king requires. I shall never see my mother or the good king, my master, again."

How long he sat there, neither I nor anybody else can tell you, but by and by he saw a little black ant creeping in through a crack in the floor. Behind it came another and another, like soldiers marching; one by one they came, till the whole floor was black with hundreds and hundreds of the ant people.

"You helped us, and we have come to help you," they said; and they set to work at once to sort the seed as the king required.

By the next day when the king came in to inquire how Hans was getting on, the work was done. The lettuce-seed was here and the radish-seed was there, the flax-seed in one corner, and the grains of rice in another; the fine seeds of flowers were in their place and the small seeds of grass were all ready for planting.

The king was astonished. He could scarcely believe his eyes; but he would not let Hans go.

"Such a fine workman must do one other piece of work before he passes through my kingdom," he said; and he took Hans out in the open country and pointed to an orchard far away.

"Bring me one golden apple that grows in that orchard and you shall go free," he said.

"Ah, what an easy task is this," said Hans, and he set off at once to the orchard.

But, alack, when he had come to the orchard gate it was guarded by a fiery dragon, the like of which he had never seen in all his life! "Come and be devoured!" it cried, as Hans came into sight.

Poor Hans! He sat down by the roadside and held his head between his hands and cried—the tears rolled down his cheeks I do assure you—for he said to himself:

"If I go into the orchard I shall be eaten alive by the dragon, and if I do not go I shall never see my mother or the good king, my master, again."

How long he sat there, neither I nor anybody else can tell you, but by and by he saw two birds flying through the air. Nearer and nearer they came till at last they reached the spot where Hans sat and lighted

THE HARPER WAS HAPPIER THAN A KING AS HE SAT
BY HIS OWN FIRESIDE.

at his feet. And they were the very birds that Hans had helped. Their wings had grown strong enough by this time to carry them wherever they wanted to go and they flapped them joyfully as they cried :

"One good turn deserves another. You helped us, and we have come to help you."

It was no trouble for them to fly into the orchard high above the dragon's head ; and almost before Hans knew they were gone they were back again bringing with them the golden apple that the king desired.

He was astonished when Hans took it to him. He could scarcely believe his eyes ; but he would not let Hans go.

Instead he took a ring from his finger and threw it to the very bottom of the sea.

"Go and fetch me that ring," he said, "and you shall be free as the birds and the bees ; but until it is upon my finger again you shall not pass through my kingdom."

Poor Hans! He sat down on the seashore and cried—the tears rolled down his cheeks I do assure you—for he said to himself:

"Who can do a task like this? I must either drown or stay here all the days of my life. I shall never see my mother or the good king, my master, again."

How long he sat there, neither I nor anybody else can tell you, but by and by three little fishes came swimming to the shore.

"One good turn deserves another," they called, for they were the very fish that Hans had thrown into the stream. "You helped us, and we have come to help you."

Then down they went to the very bottom of the sea where the king's ring lay. One of them took it in his mouth and so brought it safely to Hans who ran with it to the king.

And when the king saw the ring he knew that

ONE OF THEM TOOK IT IN HIS MOUTH, AND SO
BROUGHT IT SAFELY TO HANS.

he must let Hans go; he did not dare to keep him any longer.

So Hans mounted his horse and rode joyfully to his mother's home where he stayed till the time came when he must return to the good king, his master, which he did by another road.

He worked well and was happy serving his master faithfully, and making friends with birds and beasts, all the days of his life; but never again did he go to the wicked king's country. And I for one think he showed his good sense by that.

THE GREAT WHITE BEAR

ONCE upon a time the tailor of Wraye and the tinker of Wraye went to the king's fair together; and when they had seen all the sights that were there they started home together well pleased with their day's outing.

The sun was going down when they left the fair and when they came to the Enchanted Wood through which they had to pass the moon was rising over the hill. And a fine full moon it was, so bright that the night was almost as light as day.

"There are some people who would not venture in this wood at night even when the moon is shining," said the tinker; "but as for me I do not know what fear is."

"Nor I," said the tailor. "I would that every one had as stout a heart as mine."

And it was just then that Grandmother Grey's old white sheep that had wandered into the wood that eve came plodding through the bushes.

"Goodness me! What is that?" said the tinker clutching his companion's arm.

"A bear!" cried the tailor casting one frightened glance toward the bushes. "A great white bear! Run, run for your life."

And run they did! The tailor was small and the tinker was tall, but it was a close race between them, up hill and down hill, and into the town.

"A bear, a great white bear!" they called as they ran; and everybody they met took up the cry: "A bear, a bear!" till the whole town was roused.

The mayor and his wife, the shoemaker and his daughter, the butcher, the baker, the candlestick-maker, the blacksmith and the miller's son—indeed, to make a long story short, everybody who was awake in the town of Wraye—came hurrying out of their houses to hear what the matter was. There was soon as large a crowd as went to church on Sunday gathered about the two friends; and the tailor and the tinker talked as fast as they had run, to tell their thrilling tale.

"We were just coming through the wood," said the tailor, "when there, as close to us as the shoemaker is to the blacksmith, we saw ——"

"A terrible creature," interrupted the tinker. "'Tis as large as a calf, I assure you ——"

"And white as the mayor's shirt," cried the tailor. "It is a marvel that we escaped and if it had not been that I ——"

"I saw it first," said the tinker; "but I stood my ground. I did not run till the tailor did."

The two would have been willing to talk till morning had not all the others determined to go to the wood at once and kill the bear.

"I cannot answer for the safety of the town till it is done," said the mayor; so every one ran for a weapon as fast as his feet could carry him.

The mayor brought his long sword that the king had given him, and the carpenter a hatchet, the blacksmith took his hammer, and the miller's son a gun; and the rest of the men whatever they could put their hands on.

The women went, too, with mops and brooms to drive the bear away should he run toward the town; and one little boy who had waked up in the stir followed after them with stones in his hands.

They very soon came to the wood, and then the question was who should go first.

"Let the tinker and the tailor lead the way," said the mayor, "and we will come close after."

"Oh, no, if you please, your honor," said the tinker and the tailor speaking at the very same time. "That will never do. We cannot think of going before you."

"I will go first if the mayor will lend me his sword," said the shoemaker.

"Aye, aye, let the shoemaker go," cried some.

"No, no, 'tis the mayor's place. The king gave the sword to him," said others.

"I could kill the bear while you are talking about it," said the miller's son.

Every one had something to say, but at last it was all settled and the miller's son with the mayor's sword by his side and his own gun in his hand was just slipping into the wood when out walked the old white sheep!

"Baa, baa," she cried, as if to ask, "Pray tell me what the stir's about. Baa, baa!"

"A sheep, a sheep, a great white sheep!" cried the miller's son; and then how the people of Wraye did laugh!

They laughed and they laughed and they laughed, so loud and so long that their laughter was heard all the way to the king's fair and set the people to laughing there.

But whether the tailor and the tinker laughed or not, I do not know.

THE SONG THAT TRAVELED

ONE day when all the world was gay with spring a king stood at a window of his palace and looked far out over his kingdom. And because his land was fair to see, and he was a young king, and his heart was happy, he made a song for himself and sang it loud and merrily:

> "The hawthorn's white, the sun is bright,
> And blue the cloudless sky;
> And not a bird that sings in spring
> Is happier than I, than I,
> Is happier than I."

Now it chanced that a ploughboy at work in a field hard by the palace heard the king's song and caught the words and the air of it.

He was young and happy and as he followed his plough across the dewy field, and thought of the corn that would grow, by and by, in the furrows it made,

and of his little black and white pig that would feed
and grow fat on the corn, he sang :

> " The hawthorn's white, the sun is bright,
> And blue the cloudless sky ;
> And not a bird that sings in spring
> Is happier than I, than I,
> Is happier than I."

" A right merry song, Robin Ploughboy," called
the goose-girl who tended the farmer's geese in the
next field ; and she leaned on the fence that divided
the two, and sang with him, for she was as happy a
lass as ever lived in the king's country.

The farmer's wife had given her a goose for her very
own that day, and the goose had made a nest in the
alder bushes. There was already one egg in it and
soon there would be more. Then she would send
them to market ; and when they were sold she would
buy a ribbon for her hair. It was no wonder that she
felt like singing :

> " The hawthorn's white, the sun is bright,
> And blue the cloudless sky ;
> And not a bird that sings in spring
> Is happier than I, than I,
> Is happier than I."

The chapman,[1] from whom she bought her ribbon in all good time, learned the king's song from her; and as he trudged along the king's highway with his pack upon his back he, too, sang it; for there is no better weather for peddling or singing, either, than that which comes in the spring.

A soldier just home from the wars, and glad enough to be there, had the song from the chapman ; and in turn he taught it to a sailor who took it to sea with him.

The sailor was going to the far countries, but if all went well with his ship, and with him, he would be at home in time to see the hawthorn bloom in his mother's yard another year and another spring.

[1] A peddler.

SHE LEANED ON THE FENCE THAT DIVIDED THE TWO.

He kept the song in his heart for a year and a day, and then, because nothing had gone amiss and he was homeward bound, he sang it, too:

> " The hawthorn's white, the sun is bright,
> And blue the cloudless sky;
> And not a bird that sings in spring
> Is happier than I, than I,
> Is happier than I."

On the sailor's ship there was a minstrel bound for the king's court to sing on May Day; and the minstrel learned the song from the sailor.

He was a young minstrel and very proud to sing at the king's festival, so when it was his turn and he stood before the throne he could think of no better song to sing than:

> " The hawthorn's white, the sun is bright,
> And blue the cloudless sky;
> And not a bird that sings in spring
> Is happier than I, than I,
> Is happier than I."

Now the king had been so busy about the affairs of his kingdom deciding this question and that, sending messengers here and there, and listening to one and another, as all kings must do, that he had forgotten the song which he had made. But when he heard the minstrel it all came back to him; and then he was puzzled.

"Good minstrel," said he, "ten golden guineas I will give you for your song, and to the ten will add ten more if you will tell me where you learned it."

"An easy matter that," said the minstrel. "The sailor who rides in yon white ship in your harbor taught it to me."

"The soldier who even now stands guard at your majesty's gate gave me the song," said the sailor when he was asked.

"I had it from the chapman who travels on the king's highway," said the soldier.

"I heard the little goose-girl sing it," said the chapman when they found him.

" 'Tis Robin Ploughboy's song," laughed the goose-girl. " Go ask him about it."

" The king sang it first and I next," said the plough-boy.

Then the king knew that he had made a good song that everybody with a happy heart might sing; and because he was glad of this, he stood at his window and sang again:

THE SONG THAT TRAVELED

Words, MAUD LINDSAY   Music, ELSIE A. MERRIMAN

The hawthorn's white, the sun is bright, And blue the cloud-less sky; . And not a bird that sings in spring Is hap-pi-er than I, than I, Is hap-pi-er than I. . .

THE QUEST FOR THE NIGHTINGALE[1]

Oh, who would go to fairyland ?
The moon is shining bright, oh,
And who would go to fairyland
Upon a summer's night, oh !

Across a field of fragrant fern
All sparkling with the dew, oh !
Come trip it light to fairyland
And I will go with you, oh !

To fairyland, to fairyland,
Who seeks may find the way, oh,
And we shall see the fairies dance
Before the break of day, oh !

IN the deepest dell of the Enchanted Wood, where the moss grew the greenest and the violets bloomed the sweetest, the fairies lived.

It was they who kept the brooks and the springs

[1] I am indebted to one William Shakespeare, whose intimate acquaintance with fairyland none can dispute, for the name "Pease-Blossom"; to Joseph Rodman Drake for the idea of my story; and to some of the folk tales which suggested to me one or two of Pease-Blossom's adventures.

free from dirt or clog, and tended the wild flowers and watched over the young trees.   And they were friends with all the harmless birds and beasts from wood's end to wood's end.

But for those creatures that work harm to others, and for the goblins who delight in mischief they had no love, and every day and every night a watch was set to drive them from the fairy dell.

Each fay in turn kept guard and all went well till one evening when Pease-Blossom, the best-loved fairy in the dell, fell asleep at his post and the goblins stole away the nightingale that sang each night at the queen's court.

Great was the sorrow in fairyland when this was known.

" I will fly to catch them before they have had time to hide her away," cried a fay whose name was Quick-As-Lightning.

" I will go, too," said little Twinkle-Toes.

"And I, three," said Spice-of-Life; "and my good thorn sword with me, which will make four against them."

But the fairy queen would not consent to this.

> "Pease-Blossom in his trust did fail;
> And he must seek the nightingale,"

she said; and no sooner had she spoken than the little fay bade his companions good-bye and hastened out upon his quest alone.

The goblins had left no trace behind them and Pease-Blossom wandered hither and thither over dewy fells and fields asking of every piping cricket and brown winged bat he met: "Passed the goblins this way?"

No one could aid him, and he was ready to drop from weariness and sorrow when the moon came over the hill and called:

"Whither away, Pease-Blossom? Whither away?"

"In quest of the nightingale that the goblins have stolen ; but where they have taken her I cannot find," answered the little fay sadly.

Then said the moon : " Many a nightingale there is in the wide world, both free and caged, and how may I know yours from any other ? But this I can tell you : through a window in the castle of the Great Giant, which stands upon a high hill beside the Silver Sea, I spy a nightingale in a golden cage which was not there when I shone through that same window yester eve; and moreover, at the World's End, which is beyond the Giant's castle, I see a band of goblins counting money."

" A thousand thanks to you, oh moon," cried Pease-Blossom joyfully when he heard this; for he could put two and two together as well as any fay in fairyland, and he did not doubt that the goblins had sold the nightingale to the Great Giant.

" I shall be at the castle before you shine in the

dell," he called to the moon as he flew swift as a humming bird through the air.

But when he reached the hedge of thorns that guarded the palace of a lovely princess who was next neighbor to the Giant, he tripped against a candle-fly that was hurrying to an illumination in the palace, and tumbled headlong into the thorns.

"Help! help!" he cried as he struggled to get free, and a night-hawk that was out in a search of a supper flew down to see what the matter was.

"Oh, ho!" said he when he saw who it was. "Fairy folk like to have all things their way, but 'tis my turn now to have a little fun."

And he plucked Pease-Blossom from out the thorns and flew away with him in his bill.

Up and down, so high that the trees below looked no taller than corn stalks, and so low that their branches brushed his wings, he flew, till Pease-Blossom was faint from dizziness.

" See what a great moth the hawk has in his bill," cried an owl that they passed.

" 'Tis no moth but a bug," said a whip-poor-will.

" Such an enormous gnat should make a meal for two," whispered a brother hawk, flying close.

" Simpleton ! Do you not know a fairy when you see one ? " said the night-hawk who could keep quiet no longer.

But no sooner had he opened his bill to speak his very first word than out tumbled Pease-Blossom.

The other hawk made haste to catch the fay but before he could reach him a fine breeze came blowing by.

" Is this not my little playmate, Pease-Blossom, who likes so well to ride on the grasses and rock in the flowers ? " asked the breeze ; and it whisked the little fairy away and bore him along so fast that no bird could keep up with him.

They were at the Silver Sea in the twinkling of a star, and Pease-Blossom was just beginning to think that his troubles were ended, when the breeze died away as quickly as it had come, and the little fay found himself in the sea before he knew what was happening.

Fortunately for him a great tarpon fish came swimming by just then.

"Catch fast hold of my tail, and I will take you safely to shore," said he; and Pease-Blossom lost no time in doing as he was bid.

Ugh! How salty the water was and how the billows roared as the fish plunged through them, sending the white spray far above his head!

Poor Pease-Blossom was more dead than alive when they reached the shore, but as soon as he had gotten his breath again he said to his new friend:

"If you will come with me to fairyland you may swim in a stream as clear as glass. There is no salt in it, and no rough waves and every fairy in the dell will guard you from harm."

"Water without salt! I cannot imagine it," said the great tarpon. "And no waves! Why, I should die of homesickness there."

So when Pease-Blossom saw that there was nothing he could do for him, he thanked him kindly, and turned his steps to the Giant's castle which stood on a high hill close beside the sea just as the moon had said.

But Pease-Blossom's wings were so wet and so weary that though he tried once, twice, and thrice he could not fly to the lowest window ledge of the castle; and what he would have done nobody knows had not a chimney-swift who was out late from home flown by just then.

She lived in the castle chimney and when she heard what the little fay wanted she offered to carry him to her nest.

"Once there all will be easy," she said; "for there is no better way to get into the castle than through the chimney."

So Pease-Blossom seated himself between the swift's wings, and up they went to the top of the chimney and then down through the opening to the swift's home, which looked as if it were only half of a nest fastened against the wall.

"If you will come with me to fairyland," said Pease-Blossom when he saw this, "you shall have the greenest tree in the wood for your home. And the fairies will help you to build a whole nest there."

But the swift only laughed at him. "There is no better place than a chimney to raise young birds. I should be uneasy about them every minute in a tree. And as for a whole nest, I don't know what you mean," said she.

And when Pease-Blossom saw that she was well content with her home, he thanked her and bade her good-bye, and began his climb down the chimney.

There was no light to show him the way except the little that the moon sent through the opening high

above the swift's nest; and on all sides of the little
fay were the straight narrow walls of the chimney,
covered with black soot. He clung to them as closely
as a lichen to a rock, putting his little toes into every
crack and holding fast to the bits of cement that jutted
out here and there from the bricks. If he rustled a
wing he brought down a shower of soot upon himself,
and when at last he stood in the Giant's room, he was
as black as any goblin.

He had no time to think of himself though, for
there asleep in the golden cage which the moon had
seen was the queen's nightingale. There was no mistaking her, for there was a tiny feather missing from
the tip of her right wing, and that missing feather was
in Pease-Blossom's Sunday cap hanging in an alder
bush in the fairy dell that very minute.

The Giant was asleep, too, but the golden cage was
on a table close beside him, so close that poor Pease-
Blossom, whose wings were not improved by the soot

from the chimney, could not reach it without climbing upon the Giant's bed.

He was as careful as he could be, but no sooner had he stepped upon the bed than he touched one of the Giant's toes; and the Giant gave a great start.

"What is the matter?" called his wife.

"Oh, nothing," said he; "I only dreamed that a little mouse was tickling my toes;" and he fell asleep again.

Pease-Blossom did not dare to move till he heard him breathing heavily. Then, tiptoe across the counterpane he went, taking care at every step; but in spite of his care his wings brushed against one of the Giant's hands; and the Giant gave a great start.

"What is the matter?" called his wife.

"Oh, nothing," said he; "I only dreamed that a little leaf fell on my hand;" and he closed his eyes, and turned over on his side and was soon asleep.

Pease-Blossom was close under the cage by this time,

but so tall was the table on which it was, and so small
was he that, to reach the door, he was forced to stand
on the Giant's head.

Light as thistle-down were his feet, but no sooner
had the Giant felt their tread than he gave a great
start, and lifting his hand struck himself a tremendous
blow upon his forehead. Pease-Blossom would have
been crushed to death had he not managed to spring,
just at that instant, to the edge of the cage, where he
stood trembling.

" What is the matter ? " called the Giant's wife.

" Oh, nothing," said he ; " I only dreamed that a fly
lighted on my forehead," and he was soon breathing
heavily again.

The nightingale, who was not used to sleeping at
night, anyway, was wide awake by this time, but when
she saw Pease-Blossom she did not know him, so
black was he.

" Do you not remember the fairy dell and the little

fay to whom you gave a feather for his cap?" said Pease-Blossom then; and when the nightingale heard that, she was so overjoyed that she could scarcely keep from bursting into song.

To open the cage door was only a minute's work and the nightingale was soon as free as air. Pease-Blossom seated himself upon her back and she was just ready to fly through an open window near by when the giant waked up in real earnest and saw the open cage.

"Thieves! Robbers!" he called in such a terrible voice that the chimney-swift shook in her nest, and the big fish in the Silver Sea jumped out of the water.

If the Giant had spied Pease-Blossom and the nightingale it would have gone hard with them; but luckily for them his wife, who was a kind-hearted woman, saw them before he did, and upset the golden cage right in his way.

"The whole place is bewitched," thundered he,

STRAIGHT TO THE ENCHANTED WOOD THEY WENT.

stumbling over the cage; and in the stir which followed the nightingale slipped away unseen.

Over the Silver Sea where the fish swam, over the hedge of thorns which guarded the palace of the lovely princess, over the fields and the fells where the dew sparkled, straight to the Enchanted Wood they went.

"Who comes here?" called the fairy warder of the dell.

"Pease-Blossom and the nightingale," answered the fay; and great was the joy in fairyland at their return.

"How long you have been!" said Quick-As-Lightning.

"How fast you have come!" said little Twinkle-Toes.

But as for Spice-of-Life he could not speak at all for laughing at sooty Pease-Blossom.

Then Pease-Blossom made haste to bathe himself in the brook, and put on his finest court suit of pink satin rose-petals trimmed with lace from a spider's web; for the fairy queen had ordered a grand court ball in his honor, and there was no time to lose.

A cricket band played merrily, the nightingale sang from a thicket close at hand, and tripping and twirling the little folks went till the cock crowed and the sun came up; and it was fairy bedtime.

> In light of sun and light of moon
> How different all things seem, oh!
> Wake up, wake up, dear Sleepy Head,
> 'Twas nothing but a dream, oh.
>
> But who can tell?   Some other night
> When mellow shines the moon, oh,
> Perhaps we'll dream the dream again
> And may that night come soon, oh!

THE MAGIC FLOWER

ONCE upon a time there lived a wee woman whose bit of a garden was a delight to all eyes.

Such flowers as she had! And in the midst of them, green as an emerald and smooth as velvet, was a grass plot with never a weed upon it. And through the grass ran a garden walk as white as snow. Every one who saw it declared there was no prettier garden in the king's country and what they said was no more than what was true.

Early and late the wee woman worked to keep her garden fair and lovely but in spite of all her care whenever the east wind blew it brought with it a whirl of trash from her neighbor's dooryard, and scattered it among her flowers.

Alack and alas, what a dooryard was that! Except

for the trash that was always upon it, it was as bare as the palm of your hand; and there was a heap of dirt and ashes as high as a hillock in front of the door. Everybody who passed it turned their eyes away from it, for there was no uglier spot in the king's country; and that is nothing but the truth of it.

Whenever the wee woman looked from her windows or walked in her garden she saw the dooryard and many was the day when she said to herself:

"I wish I were a thousand miles away from it;" and if she made up her mind, as sometimes she did, that she would trouble no more about it, the east wind was sure to come with a whirl of its trash. Oh, it seemed as if she were always cleaning because of that dooryard !

And what to do about it she did not know. She puzzled and planned, she wished and she worked, but she had come to the end of her wits when, one day, her fairy godmother came to see her.

"Never fret," said the godmother when she had heard the trouble. "In your own garden grows a magic flower that can set things right; and if you will only tend it and watch it and wait long enough you shall see what you shall see."

And when she had pointed out the flower she went on her way, leaving the wee woman much comforted.

She tended the flower and watched it and waited to see what she should see; and while she was watching and waiting, the flower burst into bloom. The loveliest bloom! Every blossom was as rosy as the little clouds at sunrise; and the wee woman's garden was more beautiful than before because of them.

" 'Tis the prettiest garden in the king's country," said every one who passed; and what they said was no more than what was true.

But as for the neighbor's dooryard it was as bare and ugly as ever. The heap of dirt and ashes grew larger every day; and whenever the wind blew from the east it brought a whirl of its trash into the wee woman's garden just as it had always done.

The wee woman looked each morning to see if the magic of the flower had begun to work but morning after morning nothing changed.

"It is long waiting and weary watching for magic things to work," said she to herself; but because of what her fairy godmother had told her, she tended the flower from day to day, and hoped in her heart that something might come of it yet.

By and by the blossoms of the flower faded and fell and after them came the seed. Hundreds and hundreds of feathery seed there were, and one day the wind from the west came by, and blew them away in a whirl over the fence and into the neighbor's dooryard. No one saw them go, not even the wee woman knew what had become of them; and as for the dooryard, it was as ugly as ever with its ash heap and its

WHILE SHE WAS WATCHING AND WAITING, THE
FLOWER BURST INTO BLOOM.

trash. Everybody who passed it turned their eyes away from it.

The wee woman herself would look at it no longer.

"I will look at the magic flower instead," she said to herself, and so she did. Early and late she tended the plant and worked to make her garden fair and lovely; but she kept her eyes from the dooryard. And if the wind from the east blew trash among her flowers she raked it away and burned it up and troubled no more about it.

Summer slipped into autumn and autumn to winter and the flowers slept; but at the first peep of spring the wee woman's garden budded and bloomed once more; and one day as she worked there, with her back to the dooryard, she heard passers-by call out in delight :

"Of all the gardens in the king's country there are none so pretty as these two," and when she looked around in surprise to see what they meant she saw that

the neighbor's dooryard was full of flowers—hundreds
and hundreds of lovely blossoms, every one as rosy as
the little clouds at sunrise. They covered the heap of
dirt and ashes, they clustered about the door stone;
they filled the corners; and in the midst of them was
the neighbor, raking and cleaning as busily as if she
were the wee woman herself.

"'Tis fine weather for flowers," said she, nodding
and smiling at the wee woman.

"The finest in the world," said the wee woman; and
she nodded and smiled too, for she knew that the
magic flower had done its work.

THE LIONS IN THE WAY[1]

ONCE upon a time three friends set out to go to the palace of the king, which was known as the House Beautiful.

The king himself had invited them there, and that they might have no trouble in finding the way he sent to them a scroll upon which the path was marked so plainly that it would have been a hard matter to have missed it. And to make assurance doubly sure he wrote upon the scroll with his own hand, bidding them to keep to the path.

"Turn neither to the right nor to the left," his message said; "but follow the path and it will lead you safely to the House Beautiful, where I have prepared a place for you."

[1] Founded upon the incident of the Lions in the Way in Bunyan's "Pilgrim's Progress."

All their lives the three friends had heard of the wonders of the king's house. Some people said that it was built of gold bright as the sun itself, and others that it was made of gleaming pearl. Its windows were said to overlook the whole world, and its towers to reach higher than the sky. And every one agreed that there was naught within its gates but peace and joy.

So eager were the friends to see it that they could not journey fast enough to satisfy themselves, and from morning until night they urged each other on.

The path by which they were to go was a narrow path, with a rough place now and then, and now and then a briar or sharp stone upon it, but for the most part it was a pleasant way. The travelers hastened joyfully along it and all went well with them until, one day, they met a man whose face was turned toward the land from which they had just come.

"Good neighbors," he cried, "why travel you so fast? Is a house afire or a friend ill; or does a feast wait till you come? Tell me, I pray you, that I may sorrow with you, or rejoice, as your need may be."

"Rejoice, rejoice!" cried the three; "for we journey to the king's House Beautiful, where a place is prepared for us."

But when the man heard this he shook his head sorrowfully as if what they told him was grievous news indeed.

"I, too, had thought of going there," he said; "but that was before I knew of the lions in the way."

"Lions in the way!" cried the travelers, looking at each other with startled eyes.

"Aye, lions," repeated the man solemnly, "the fiercest and largest that ever man saw. Their very roaring shakes the ground, and many a traveler has been devoured by them, so people say. As for myself, I have not seen them. To hear of them is enough for me."

"And for me," said one of the travelers; and in spite of all his companions might do or say to persuade him, he would go no farther.

"The king's house may be beautiful as the morning and as full of wonders as the sky is full of stars, but what good will it be to me if I am eaten by the lions?" said he.

And his friends were forced to journey on without him.

As they went they talked of the lions in the way and the one said to the other:

"Think you it is true, or but an idle tale?"

"True or not we shall pass in safety. Have we not the king's own word for it?" said the other; and he led the way with such great strides that his friend could scarcely keep pace with him.

On and on they traveled without stop or hindrance,

till all at once the air was filled with a great noise that shook the earth beneath their feet and set their knees to trembling.

There was no mistaking what it was. Even though they had never heard the sound before, they knew it was the roaring of the lions.

And the second traveler began to grow afraid.

"Let us go around by another way," he said. "Surely there are more paths than one to the king's house."

And though the other spread out before him the scroll on which the path was marked and read once more the message of the king: "Turn neither to the right nor to the left but follow the path and it will lead you safely to the House Beautiful, where a place is prepared for you," he would pay no heed to it but turned away into a by-path and followed it out of sight.

The other traveler was forced to journey on the path

alone, with the roaring of the lions in his ears and the shaking of the earth beneath his feet. Nor had he gone a furlong more when just ahead he spied the lions themselves. One on each side of the path they stood with flaming eyes and yawning mouths; and at the very sight of them the traveler's heart beat quick and sharp and his feet faltered upon the way.

But his faith in the king's word was greater than his fear. "Falter not, oh, feet! Fear not, oh, heart! There is safety in the path. The king himself has said it," he cried as he pressed on.

And lo! and behold, when he had come to the lions he found that they were chained. Roar as they might and strive as they would, they could not touch those who walked in the path that the king had marked; and the traveler passed in safety.

Beyond the lions stood the House Beautiful, with walls of gold bright as the sun itself and gates of gleaming pearl. Its windows overlooked the world,

WHEN HE HAD COME TO THE LIONS HE FOUND
THAT THEY WERE CHAINED.

its towers reached above the sky, and of its wonders not the half had ever been told him.

The traveler's place was prepared for him, and the king was waiting to welcome him to his house; and he lived there in peace and joy forever after.

THE END

aa

CPSIA information can be obtained
at www.ICGtesting.com
Printed in the USA
LVHW081301071020
668195LV00013B/107